TALL SKINNY BITTER

Notes from the Center of Coffee Culture

Dani Cone & Chris Munson

SASQUATCH BOOKS
SEATTLE

Printed in Singapore by Star Standard Industries Pte Ltd
Published by Sasquatch Books
Distributed by PGW/Perseus
15 14 13 12 11 10 09   9 8 7 6 5 4 3 2 1

Front cover illustration/photograph: Chris Munson
Back cover illustration: Leigh Riibe
Cover design: Chris Munson
Interior design and illustrations: Chris Munson,
   Jean Bradbury, Aileen Morrow, and Leslie Riibe
Interior composition: Chris Munson

*Special thanks to all the baristas, managers, and roasters who
provided photographs and gave us their permission to use them.*

ISBN-10: 1-57061-565-9
ISBN-13: 978-1-57061-565-8

Sasquatch Books
119 South Main Street, Suite 400
Seattle, WA 98104
(206) 467-4300
www.sasquatchbooks.com
custserv@sasquatchbooks.com

Introduction

Twenty years ago or less, if you started a sentence with "My barista said . . ." people would look at you as if you'd just referenced an insightful tip from your pet rock. Nowadays such an opener can make you sit up and listen, really tune in to the rest of the sentence—after all, who has their finger on the pulse more than a barista?

The importance of the barista's role in society is evidenced in the possessive people often use with the word: *my* barista, *our* barista, and the like. There is a personal connection that we don't often see in this generic, computer-based world. Baristas foster this connection in many ways, and sometimes it's the most personal interaction someone will have during the entire day! *Your* barista is quite possibly the first person you see each day, setting the tone while giving you not just your morning ritual in a cup, but the time, weather, much-needed fashion advice, music to wake you up, a listening ear, helpful advice, directions, solicited and/or unsolicited opinions, daily news, gossip, political analysis, art and movie reviews, friendship—and of course, coffee. We didn't just get clout, we *earned* it. And it certainly hasn't happened overnight.

The coffee industry has grown exponentially in the past two decades, especially here in the Northwest. From the '80s "cart wars" in Seattle to the present-day big-chain omnipresence and the impressive momentum of indie coffee shops, specialty coffee has definitely proven to be an exciting and kinetic marketplace. Each day is abuzz with new technologies, refinements, techniques, and more along each step of the process from farm to mug. Growers, pickers, processors, buyers, traders, distributors, roasters, and baristas expertly share the helm and contribute their knowledge and skill to each cup. Baristas are the final word in this process. And we often act accordingly.

This book is a "showcase showdown" of barista and coffee shop style. Coffee began as a commodity industry and has over time produced a culture. *Tall Skinny Bitter* illustrates coffee shops in Seattle and Portland, providing insight, advice, trivia, funny stories, everything you ever wanted to know about coffee but were afraid to ask, and an inside look at the barista profession and its culture. It is a chance to get a glimpse of life behind the counter: the fashion, the music, the facts, the quips, the love of the bean.

Plus, think of this book as a guide to the coolest indie coffeehouses in the Northwest. In these pages, you can learn about such things as how to make the perfect latte, the number of cups a coffee shop goes through in a year, and the new trend of direct-trade relationships between coffeehouses and coffee bean growers. Sprinkled throughout are visual profiles of the diverse indie coffeehouses in the Northwest and the baristas who make each place so special.

I have been a barista for 17 years now, and I've seen so much growth and development in what for me started as just a job but became a career. I shudder to think of the first latte I made and sincerely offer my apologies to that unfortunate customer. It was the early '90s and the only coffee job in my area was at a deli; coffee was an afterthought at best. So I alternated between slicing meat and making espresso drinks, and I became hooked on the latter. Though I tested the waters in other fields and even briefly entertained jobs that required suits and expense accounts, I knew there was only one job for me that would allow me to spend my working hours in the sort of place I spend my free time. More often than not I found myself reveling in the fact that I was actually getting paid to meet amazing people, learn about coffee, prepare drinks, and generally have a lot of fun.

I worked at some good cafés and a few great ones before deciding to open my own shop, Fuel. Yep, March 30, 2005, I officially turned myself entirely over to the world of coffee and haven't looked back since. I half-expected a badge or something. I mean, I didn't need a ticker-tape parade or anything, but a trumpet or two would've been nice. Instead, here's what I got: drier skin, more calluses, browner coffee stains on my hands, cushier shoes, a whole new set of only dark-colored shirts (it's tough to keep a white shirt looking good while working behind the bar), steam wand burns, and coffee grounds turning up in really odd places. But most importantly, I seriously fell in love all over again with what I do and who I do it with. The coffee and the customers are what get me up each day and make me realize that this is the greatest job on earth.

Baristas really experience it all: hilarity, nightmares, early-morning dramas, late-night crimes, crazy requests, angry demands, costumes, holidays, midweek weekends, afternoon naps, propositions, gifts, free concert tickets, free meals, free you-name-it in the barista bartering scene, and so, so much more. If I hadn't been a barista, when else in my life would I have really gotten threatened with an *actual sword* in Seattle? Or how would I have found some of my favorite books and best friends? We experience a lot, we see a lot, and we even get a lot. In return, we give all of ourselves to our work. There is no other time in my life when I actually raise my voice a few octaves to sound friendlier than when I'm behind the bar. At work, I'm willing to give that and more. A million times more.

A barista is more than just the person who is working behind the bar at a coffee shop. Dedicated baristas explore the craft of coffee with skill and an insatiable thirst for knowledge. This field changes and is refined daily, and a barista must keep up with the latest developments while maintaining a keen sense of artistry and tradition. These days baristas go beyond their shifts and cafés and meet and exchange ideas at international conferences, trade shows, competitions, and Internet sites. This book celebrates coffeehouse life and the baristas who make it happen. Who knows, it may be a significant step in legitimizing the notion of a "career barista," or maybe we'll even get a Barista Appreciation Day on the calendar. I am particularly excited to bring even a fraction of barista lifestyle to the forefront of the public's mind and to also provide baristas with a look into each other's lives and a reminder of why we love what we do.

Who else but baristas can successfully do three things at once while carrying on an in-depth conversation against the siren song of a squealing steam wand, a whirring grinder, the incessant bell of the cash register, and the morning soundtrack?

Your barista,
Dani Cone

THE Albina PRESS

**NORTH PORTLAND
SE PORTLAND**

BILLY is an award-winning industry celeb barista of six years. "I love it. I got into it for the coffee itself and my interest in that. The coffee industry has been around for hundreds of years, but it still feels new. There are always so many things changing each day in the coffee industry, new technologies and developments, and it's great how that mingles with the history and age of coffee itself."

BEN: "I've been a barista for three years here." The best part of the job? "For me, it's the social aspect, hanging out and cracking jokes. For them, it's working with me!"

Ben, the manager

Kevin, the owner. He has been a barista for 4 years, since opening Albina Press.

Nicole, barista

Against the backdrop of barista trophies behind the bar, there is an easy camaraderie among the crew. Humor, skill, and wit fly around almost as fast as customers pour in—but the baristas never miss a beat. While tearing through a huge line of drinks, they laugh, chat, and engage the customers (and each other) with stories of last night's outings, tip jar theft, allusions to a "long story" about the crack in the back door, and more. Obvious professionalism with true Portland-style humility and grace.

ALL CITY COFFEE
GEORGETOWN ~ PIONEER SQUARE ~ SEATTLE WA
Guaranteed Fresh

Constantly maintained buzz/permanent aura of stale-coffee-reek.

Job perks/hazards?

If you weren't a barista what would you be doing?
I'd be working in a cubicle somewhere, god forbid.

Hobbies/interests?

I read manuscripts for a literary agency and copyedit for an online lit magazine.

Paige (5 years)

8:15 a.m. Saturday morning,

listening to Badly Drawn Boy

GEORGETOWN & PIONEER SQUARE

Who's Who in the Coffee Shop

Baristas

- Passionate about all things coffee (a coffee geek—in a good way!)

- People person/social butterfly

- People person/social butterfly who would actually rather be working in a bar but got in trouble at his or her last bartender job for matching customers shot for shot

- Morning person: unbelievably chipper and functional at 5 a.m.

- Hepcat: classic barista, probably a musician/writer/artist, sometimes filled with charming angst

- "I'm a musician/artist/writer and I need a day job."

- "I'm here to meet cute boys/girls—and oh yeah, make coffee."

- "This is my career and I'm truly passionate about coffee. Coffee = life."

- "I have a degree and can't find a job."

- "I make more as a barista than I could with my degree."

- "I love people."

Customers

- The regular, the semiregular, the "I want you to treat me like a regular but I'm not" guy

- The competitor: vies for being the most regular regular—and wants recognition for it

- The customer who used to be or thinks he or she is a barista

- The name-dropper

- The coffee geek

- The coffee show-off

- "Your team": a customer a barista designates to be a coworker's hypothetical teammate, because you wouldn't want him or her on your team

- High-maintenance: the customer who asks for too many variables in an order or is too specific (e.g., one-third of a shot of vanilla, 1 inch of foam, a half inch of room)

- Tall nonfat vanillas: Admit it—you can spot these folks a mile away.

How to Make Coffee Drinks

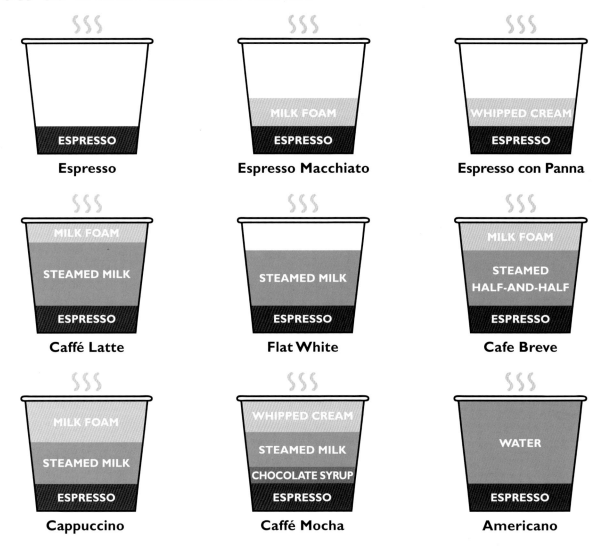

FINE COFFEE • DESSERTS

B&O

SINCE 1976

SEATTLE • 322-5028

ESPRESSO

CAPITOL HILL

Aleah, a barista of six years, is listening to classical music.

"My best advice for a new barista is to try all the drinks, and be careful of tendonitis! When I'm working, the best part of the job is the people I work with, and when I'm not at work, I enjoy painting and video/film art."

Olympia WA

Dancing Goats Espresso Company opened in 1988 as a café that featured espresso drinks and desserts. Two years later owners Larry and Cherie purchased a small coffee house, Batdorf & Bronson, that also had a burgeoning wholesale division.

Batdorf & Bronson Coffee Roasters has grown to include a roastery in Atlanta, GA, a new roasting facility in Olympia, and six retail and licensed locations. Batdorf & Bronson is also a 100% green company: All of their electricity comes from renewable resources, solar energy helps power the computer systems, and recycling and composting programs keep 30,000 pounds of refuse out of the landfill each year.

Van, one of Batdorf & Bronson's premier coffee roasters, has been with the company since 1991.

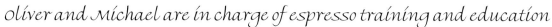

Oliver and Michael are in charge of espresso training and education

OLIVER, barista for 16 years!

Each new barista goes through barista certification training of 60 hours. The training goes beyond pouring a perfect drink as they also focus on the seed to cup process, cupping, training with the roasters, and more.

I've been a barista for about 5 years but I would say 3 years professionally... that is since I started working here! — Sasha

JEN, the marketing manager.

MICHAEL— barista for 15 years!

Coffee by the Numbers

Number of coffeehouses in the Seattle area: 628 (or 2.5 shops per every 10,000 residents)

Number of coffeehouses in the Portland area: 419 (or 2 shops per every 10,000 residents)

Range in tips per day: $10–$90

Average working hours for a barista: 6 hrs/day, 4–5 days/wk; about 24–30 hrs/wk

Roughly what a small Seattle coffee shop goes through in a year of business:
- 72,457 paper cups
- 15,355 pastries
- 6,205 labor hours
- 4,188 pounds of coffee
- 2,975 gallons of milk
- 621 dog biscuits
- 54 members of the shop-dog's fan club
- 18 players on the shop's softball team
- 7 dedicated baristas
- 2 employee parties

What few words describe you as a barista?
Nice, bearded

Worst drink you've ever made?
Blueberry cappuccino

Why is this the best job ever?
You meet amazing people. We are like a big family.

What is your favorite/least favorite part of the job?
Fave: People
Boo: Mean people

Advice for a new barista?
Be nice. It's not that hard.

—Tyler

bauhaus books + coffee
seattle CAFFEINE

CAPITOL HILL

YOU MEET AMAZING PEOPLE WE ARE LIKE A BIG FAMILY

Tyler, barista for 6 years
Grace, barista for 13 years

Bird on a Wire

West Seattle

Heidi's team!

Derby champs!

Coffee-table reading

HEIDI,

owner of Bird on a Wire, got her first barista job in 1986 while working in a bakery/café. "They brought in a small, awkward-looking espresso machine and we all stood around and said 'We don't know what that is but it tastes nasty and nobody wants it!'"

But she was hooked. As her knowledge and experience grew, she thought, *I should just do this.* And, six years ago, she did. Bird on a Wire opened in 2002, and Heidi has been rewarded in many ways by her supportive, warm, and welcoming neighborhood—one that has made her often feel like a local celebrity.

When she's not busy behind the bar Heidi also maintains a landscaping business and serves as captain of the Rat City Rollergirls roller derby team Grave Danger—call her Skate Trooper in the rink.

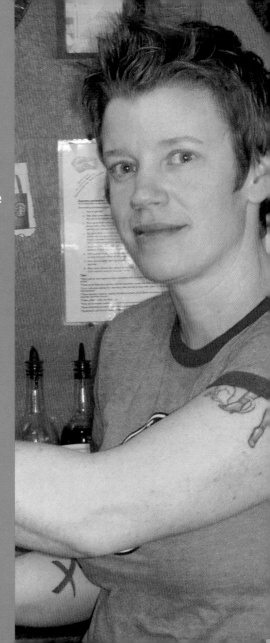

BUS STOP ESPRESSO

1
2
3 10th Drink
4 **FREE**
5
6
7 Roosevelt

Tips!

LEVI

a true artist

BRIDGET

loud and scattered

One of the most memorable drinks I've made is a 20-oz, 6-shot raspberry—white chocolate mocha with whip and caramel sauce on top—or a single 20-oz dry capp.

If I wasn't a barista I'd be sculpting—and starving. —Levi

Ask Dani

Q. *Dani, is it possible to make a great cup of coffee from Folgers or Sanka?*

A. I posed this question to a number of fellow baristas. A resounding "no" could be heard from the barista masses! Or at least a "not really." For starters, there is a difference in the beans used, arabica (used most often by coffeehouses) versus robusta (once thought of as inferior, though now enjoying somewhat of a comeback; common in brand-name coffee). Next, to create coffeehouse-quality coffee, baristas prepare drinks with beans that are ground to order—never preground—and this ensures the highest quality and freshness: a huge step above freeze-dried coffee! Not to mention the joyous benefit of having your personally crafted drink versus a coffee that is packaged for the masses. There is an entire journey of the bean from seed to cup, and each step along the way is an important part of the quality. From the soil in which the coffee plants grow to the distribution, roasting, packaging, grinding, dosing, pulling, and extraction, your latte has truly been through a ritualistic and multifaceted process, and is celebrated in the hands of professionals. Here's an analogy: You can buy a cool T-shirt off a rack of 20 of the same ones at a big-box store, and you'll be guaranteed they'll have five of your size and maybe it will even be on sale. Not bad. Or you can seek out an indie designer who's created a unique screenprint and know you're getting something perfectly handcrafted and special—and probably better quality too, since it's a much more hands-on experience and process.

Q. *Is it true that coffee has medicinal qualities?*

A. Coffee has a rich, centuries-old history in the medicinal field. Though unconfirmed in many traditional Western practices, coffee can be used to aid respiratory, gastric, and digestive health. Coffee also staves off prolonged mental fatigue and sleep. It can increase reflex response time and mental activity, too. It has been widely reported that a moderate quantity of coffee is not only not harmful, but can even be beneficial. It's no secret that coffee stimulates the body and mind, but as is true of other stimulants, too much can act as a depressant. Because of its stimulating qualities, coffee is often regarded as an aphrodisiac—so go ahead and make it a triple shot!

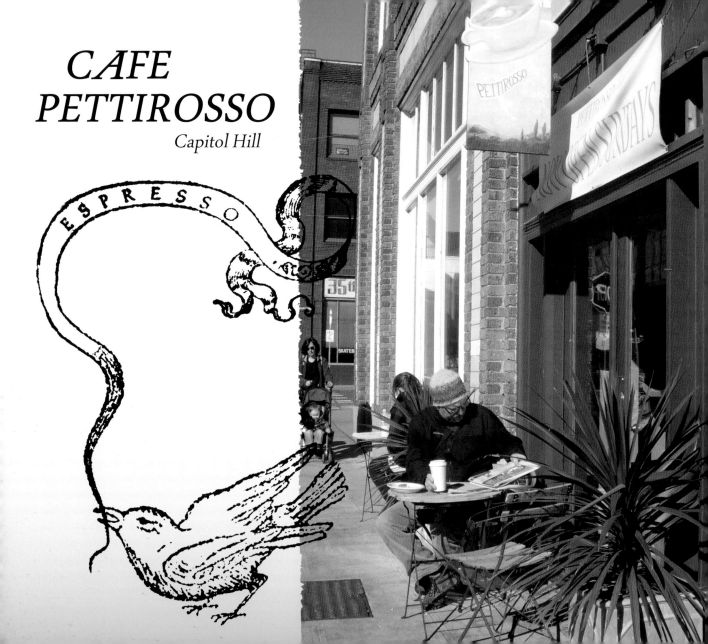

CAFE PETTIROSSO

Capitol Hill

ESPRESSO

Robin opened her cart in the original REI building in Seattle in 1989. She had been looking for a career change of sorts and focused on what she liked best: coffee and Italy. Robin's husband is from Vienna, a place with a strong coffee culture and an appreciation of the tradition and ritual of making coffee. When Robin's Espresso's opened, carts were easy to get into and were some of the best sources of coffee in Seattle.

In 1996, Robin decided to grow her cart operation into a café. Robin's Espresso became Cafe Pettirosso. "At that time, there were three or four other coffee shops in the entire Capitol Hill area—and I thought that was saturated!" Robin remembers. Now Capitol Hill has one of the highest concentrations of coffee shops in Seattle, literally almost one on every block, if not more. But Robin welcomes the variety and realizes that there are plenty of people with plenty of different tastes to support all sorts of cafés. "The more the merrier!" she says.

Pettirosso is a sunny, cozy local favorite, always buzzing with activity and offering amazing coffee, breakfast and lunch fare, and pies to write home about.

Robin   **Yuki**   **Danell**

Caffé Appassionato

Photo: Rob Wiek

Gary Kelfner, owner: I own possibly the smallest coffee shop in Seattle. At 62 square feet, there is not a lot of space to work with, no room for even a chair! Every square foot has something essential to doing business. I set up shop every morning and Lauren breaks it down every night. It's a lot of work, but it's so much fun that it's well worth it. Rent is high, taxes take a big bite, costs are rising every month, but the joy of seeing the same people every day, talking about their day and what's important to them, makes it so worthwhile. I have a front row seat on the world of University Way. Almost every day I say, "Well, now I've seen it all!" Along comes the next day, and something different happens. I've seen countless drug deals, car wrecks, fights, acts of kindness, naked women walking down the middle of the street. Right upstairs is KUOW, Public Radio. Through those doors have

walked many important people, from Bill Gates to the mayor of Seattle. Every week I ask them, "Who's coming around this week?" I LOVE my coffee shop. Evey day is different, every day I make a new coffee. Today I made an extra-dry, nonfat, CHERRY cappuccino! What's going to happen tomorrow?

Lauren Bachman, manager: My customers, especially the regulars, are what make my job so enjoyable. The problem customers are few and far between and when they do come along, they're always followed by someone who makes me forget the difficulties. I've grown a lot as a person, into a young adult, in part due to my regulars. We've given each other advice and support and it shows in the way we converse, give each other gifts, and learn from one another.

Specialty Drinks

It's commonly believed that Northwest baristas frown upon specialty flavors and coffees. Not true! Here are some popular specialty drinks you can discover around the region:

Almond Joy: almond and vanilla mocha
Go Away: single grande nonfat cappuccino with flavoring
London Fog: Earl Grey tea steeped in steamed milk with vanilla
Milky Way: caramel vanilla mocha
Polar Bear: white chocolate mocha with vanilla
Red Eye/Yankee Dog/Whiz/All-Nighter: drip coffee with a shot of espresso in it
Sweet Pink: raspberry white chocolate mocha
Van Halen: vanilla and hazelnut latte
Why Bother: single short decaf nonfat latte

A Word about Macchiatos

By Rebecca Haberkorn (barista of 1½ years)

Shortly after beginning my current job at a local independent coffee shop, I learned part of a secret code: Starbucks lingo. It's a language unto itself, and it often needs to be translated for us unsuspecting baristas at the little local shops, all of whom speak a related (but not equivalent) vernacular. Where I work, our smallest size is a short, not a tall. In a similar vein, our largest is not a vente, it's a grande. It may seem like a small point, but in all honesty I do not enjoy negotiating around the expectation that we would conform to the standards set by another business. Particularly one with which we compete.

My largest beef is with the word "macchiato." If you order a macchiato, I'll take it to mean that you want two shots of espresso "marked" with steamed milk. However, at Starbucks, as I came to learn, "macchiato" is another word for caramel latte, for reasons I can't fathom.

And as you might imagine, the first macchiato that I made for a native Starbucks speaker was completed to satisfaction only on the second attempt.

But it got me thinking, and I noticed an opportunity to glean something of a customer's meaning from the way she or he orders a drink. If the order starts with "short," "tall," or "grande," then it must be a macchiato of the caramel latte variety, since a traditional marked macchiato is served in a teensy 2-oz cup with no variation in size. But if the order has no size-differential adjectives attached, then I would just have to use my best judgment. (Many people forget to mention a size when they first place their order, so "I'll have a macchiato" is not a guarantee that I know what the customer means.) Now you'd think it would be easy to ask the question, "Do you mean a macchiato in a small cup like this, or do you mean a caramel latte?" But I have been met with displays of exquisite intellectual snobbery—or conversely, painful confusion—for asking that very question, and my blood boils just thinking about Starbucks and its meaningless macchiato madness.

So I try not to ask that question. I avoid it at all costs. Is it illogical? Perhaps, but to that I respond: It is far worse for Starbucks to call a caramel latte a "macchiato." And sometimes it is obvious to me what the customer intends (which kind of coffee culture might she or he be used to?). If it's not obvious, I communicate in subtle ways. For instance, setting up the cup in a prominent position so that if it happens to be the wrong type, I'll find myself corrected before the damage is done (I usually accompany this by the question, "For here or to go?" to bring extra attention to the cup).

That was my strategy for many weeks. It worked, until one day I found myself face to face with a customer who threw a wrench into the whole complex machinery.

She was clever, all right. Quite the poker face. I had no reason to expect what would come next.

"I'll have a macchiato in a short cup."

I smiled, thinking, a short caramel latte, you say? I'm on it, and moved to the cash register to ring in her order before setting up the drink.

Now I was in her trap, and unwittingly so. I recited the price back to her, but too late—all too late.

"That's not right. Your menu says a macchiato is $2.15."

"Oh, that's for a traditional macchiato, espresso with a little steamed milk. But you want a caramel latte, right?"

"No. I want a macchiato, but in one of your short cups, only partly full. I don't want it to spill. You can do that, right?"

I don't think she had ever been to Starbucks, because she was looking at me awfully strangely.

Foiled again! I cursed inwardly as I explained the source of the confusion. How I loathe that white and green!

The only thing left for me to do was to restore her confidence in my abilities by making sure her macchiato "in a short cup" was extra delicious.

CAFFÉ FIORÉ
OLD BALLARD, SUNSET HILL & QUEEN ANNE

JOSEPH

WHAT FEW WORDS DESCRIBE YOU AS A BARISTA? A WINK AND A SMILE. FAVORITE DRINK TO MAKE? ANY DRINK 8 OZ OR LESS. WORST DRINK YOU'VE EVER MADE? I DON'T MAKE BAD DRINKS. ADVICE FOR A NEW BARISTA? LEARN TO LOVE THE AFTERNOON NAP. JOB PERKS/ HAZARDS? PERKS: FREE COFFEE HAZARDS: REPETITIVE STRESS INJURIES. HOBBIES/INTERESTS? MUSIC & ART WITH DIRT IN ITS TEETH. IF YOU WEREN'T A BARISTA WHAT WOULD YOU BE DOING? PUMPING GAS OR ROLLING BURRITOS MAYBE. WHY IS THIS THE BEST JOB EVER? REVOLUTIONS START IN COFFEE SHOPS. —JOSEPH

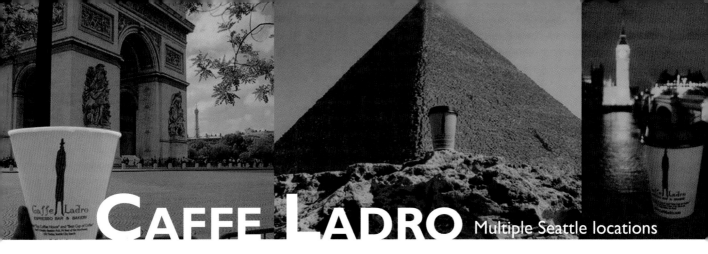

CAFFE LADRO
Multiple Seattle locations

Caffe Ladro is many things to many people. It is a place to come for—of course—coffee and pastries. A place to sit, read, work on a laptop, meet people, create new friendships, experience life …

As the store manager of the Union Street Caffe Ladro I insist that everyone have fun, experience life, serve and receive great coffee and service. This includes baristas, customers, vendors, AND the store manager. In this world of the internet, e-mail, and text messaging, the opportunity to communicate in person becomes ever so much more valuable, precious. My hopes for any café is for a person to walk in as a customer and hopefully leave as a friend. In the downtown café friendships grow out of a 30-second to one minute conversation five days a week, month after month, hopefully year after year. In this process a café is given the opportunity to host hundreds of people on a daily basis. When you think about that, it is truly a gift. The café is where life comes to you, happens, and if you are paying attention you get to partake.

The photos on this page are tokens of those friendships. If you asked a friend to take your favorite paper coffee cup with them on their travels abroad and photograph them at their destination they would do this. Our friends have.

—David Narazaki, store manager

LONDON ✈ PARIS ✈ VIENNA ✈ FRANKFURT ✈ BUDAPEST ✈ MOSCOW ✈ PROVENCE ✈ CAIRO ✈ POSITANO ✈ CRE

Faves: free coffee, being sassy and skilled, phone numbers in the tip jar, neighborhood notoriety, great customer/barista relationships.

Not-so-faves: anything blended, dry skin, early hours, drinks with more than six adjectives or fractions. Plus, caramel macchiatos are not real drinks!

Specific way to order a drink: size does matter, "please" and "thank you" do too!

New barista advice: Don't take it personally.

Desiree (10 years)

Kevin (4 years)

Sarah (3 years)

JOHANNESBURG ✈ ATHENS ✈ LUSAKA ✈ ISTANBUL

Are You a Serious Coffee Drinker?

In a highly unscientific poll, we asked Northwest baristas what coffee drink orders distinguish "serious" coffee drinkers from lame ones. Though the idea of ranking coffee drinks in the Northwest is highly subjective, we found common results. The following list represents where your coffee drink stands in the ranks:

1. Doppio or macchiato (a traditional macchiato that is, not the bastardized version!)
2. Cappuccino—8 oz, of course
3. Americano
4. Drip
5. Latte
6. Breve
7. Mocha, or anything with a flavor
8. Anything with multiple variables
9. Flavored drip coffee

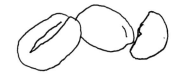

CAFFÈ UMBRIA®

COFFEE ROASTING COMPANY

PIONEER SQUARE (SEATTLE) &
PEARL DISTRICT (PORTLAND)

Kaci (café manager)

IN 1948 ORNELLO BIZZARRI BEGAN the family tradition of roasting Italian coffees in his hometown of Perugia, Italy. His son Umberto brought that tradition to Seattle in 1986, starting the Torrefazione Italia coffe company, roasting and serving his coffee from a Pioneer Square location. Though the Torrefazione cafés have closed, Ornello's grandson Emanuele continues the family tradition with Caffé Umbria. Its flagship café is located where Torrefazione's flagship once stood, and Emanuele invites all coffee drinkers in to experience *il Gusto del Caffé.*

Multiple locations in Seattle and Olympia

That coffee in your cup is the result of a long, complex journey. A barista is its last stop, and with skill and knowledge we deliver the potential that was planted half a world away. We know how the smallest change in preparation can compromise the taste of the drink we serve. A delicate balance must be acheived for the optimal extraction of flavor and aroma from this volatile bean. But we should not forget that we are only one part of this story.

I learned this on a trip I took to the origin of some of our beans. Under a dense canopy of sweltering humidity in Guatemala a new fascination took hold of me, a fascination with the life and death of the fruit coffea, and its rebirth as a coffee bean. The farm I visited, which dated back to the turn of the 20th century, provided the inspiration. I inhaled the perfume of allspice, vanilla, peppercorns, and cardomom growing around me. A crystalline stream of water wound its way from the jungle to the tanks where the coffee fruit was washed, sorted, processed, and then dried.

Organic farming relies on healthy soil, and Señor Alex was only too happy to shove handfuls of warm compost up to our surprised noses. He explained how the shade trees must all be cropped to allow the right amount of sunlight at the right time to his precious plants. We talked about microclimates that exist in different parts of the farm, resulting in different coffees. The world of coffee is infinitely complex.

Back in Seattle, Caffé Vita is now buying coffee from this farm, directly from those who care about it intimately. I am convinced that this is the way it should be, and that the future of quality coffee depends on these sorts of relationships. We have extended our love beyond the cupping, roasting, and brewing, to the place where it matters the most, the origin.

—Daniel Shewmaker

Caffé Vita and Direct Trade

By Mason Sager

For 3 years, I have worked as a coffee roaster for Caffé Vita, an artisanal, locally owned, independent coffee-roasting company in Seattle, Washington. We roasters are a small bunch, dedicated to roasting and serving exceptional coffee. As a coffee roaster for Caffé Vita, I have the incredible opportunity to be involved in sourcing, purchasing, roasting, and cupping some of the world's finest coffee. Coffee sourced, roasted, and served at Caffé Vita is from the major coffee-producing regions around the world, including Central America, South America, Africa, and Indonesia. Caffé Vita is dedicated to serving exceptional coffee and understands that this commitment extends further than our own cafés. It takes us to the coffee farms and allows us to meet the people who are directly responsible for producing exceptional coffee. This is exciting to me because it allows me to learn about the deeper backstory of coffee, that of coffee as an agricultural product deeply rooted in many sociopolitical and environmental issues. Land-use management, sustainable and organic farming practices, ethical labor standards, and the economics of trading/purchasing coffee are issues that impact the quality and availability of coffee and add to the complexity and texture of the coffee world.

As a coffee roaster, I am interested in the agricultural side of coffee and the relationship between the coffee farmer and the coffee roaster. I believe it is important for the coffee roaster, and consumers of coffee in general, to have an understanding of and appreciation for the tremendously laborious task of producing the green coffee bean that we roast and ultimately consume. I am interested in the unique agricultural practices of each individual farm and the relationship between the coffee farmer and the coffee plant. I want to know about the amount of care and dedication that went into producing the coffee and how this effort shapes the lives and culture of the farmers. I am interested in the relationship between the coffee farmer and the land that he or she farms, which will certainly lead me to explore and understand the geography and natural history of coffee-producing countries. Coffee has such a deep-rooted, rich history, and I am excited about the opportunity to experience places like Guatemala, Peru, Brazil, Ethiopia, Kenya, Rwanda, Java, and Sumatra, and learn about how the unique socioeconomic and environmental issues of each country/region contribute to the richness and complexity found in each individual cup of coffee.

I believe that our stance on all of the societal issues surrounding coffee is defined and supported by our purchasing practices. This is a shared vision at Caffé Vita and was the impetus for creating Caffé Vita Farm Direct Coffee. This coffee allows us to travel the world to source out exceptional beans from all the major coffee-producing regions and purchase the coffee directly from the coffee farmer or co-op. In addition to the quality of coffee being exceptional, we are also looking for coffee farms that implement responsible land use and have healthy/viable working and living conditions. In essence, Caffé Vita is purchasing coffee above fair-trade prices from producers who are committed to producing exceptional coffee without compromising quality, environmental responsibility/stewardship, and human rights. Directly supporting coffee farmers, not coffee bureaucracy.

Caffé Vita roasts blends as well as single-origin varietals at varying degrees of light to dark roast in order to highlight and display the inherent characteristics of each bean. I find enjoyment in understanding the different nuances of the individual coffees and how the coffee responds to the heat intensity and the duration of the roast. For instance, our Caffé Vita Farm Direct Finca Nuevo Viñas from Guatemala is a high-elevation, strictly hard-bean coffee that is rather delicate and requires a light roast, which will not distort or overpower the delicate nuances of the bean. Contrast this to our organic Sumatra Mandheling, which lends itself better to a darker, more intense roast that highlights its robust, earthy smoke/spice components. Therefore, it is the bean that determines the roast, and it is up to the roaster to identify and apply the appropriate roast for the inherent qualities of the individual bean.

The relationship between the coffee farmer and coffee roaster is paramount in producing exceptional coffee. Understanding the intricacies involved in the agricultural process of coffee gives me a greater respect for the coffee I roast and for the lives coffee impacts throughout the world. I am very honored to roast coffee for Caffé Vita and am excited about my involvement with Caffé Vita Farm Direct coffee. I feel that it gives us the opportunity to bring to Seattle not only exceptional coffee from around the world, but stories of the lives of the farmers who produce the coffee. It also further educates consumers of coffee about the issues surrounding this amazing crop, which produces such a wonderfully luxurious drink.

Brooke, a barista of 6½ years, is listening to an '80s mix CD. "My best advice to a new barista is to love what you do. This job is so much fun, and I love that we can dance on our shift and just be ourselves. The only problems come when tables get in the way of our dance party!"

eats

Maple Leaf

Cloud City Coffee

Ask Dani

Q. *Dani, does the coffee I drink around town come from the Northwest?*

A. You would think so! Or at least we would. Actually, coffee's brief history goes like this:

Legend has it that sometime around AD1000, an East African goat herder (or sheep herder, jury's out on this one) became surprised by the unusual behavior of his herd after they munched on some peculiar berries. The goats became more energetic and frisky. Kaldi, the goat herder, inspected the berry bush and, trying a few of the berries himself, also felt a burst of energy. Not surprisingly, many religious leaders of the time quickly deemed the plant a product of the devil. Others, however, embraced the discovery and soon began collecting the berries, drying them, and transporting them back to the monasteries. There they were placed in water to revive the flavor, and the new stimulant was used to prepare monks for daily prayer.

In subsequent centuries, coffee was regarded as a drink for medicinal and ritual purposes and was held as a closely guarded secret. In the latter half of the 15th century, the first coffee shop opened in Constantinople. European traders then began importing the bean, and in the 17th and 18th centuries, coffeehouses sprung up in Italy, London, Paris, Vienna, and Berlin. The magical combination of coffee and conversation was born. The Enlightenment era embraced this idea and cultivated it. Coffeehouses became informal forums for thinkers, artists, and political and social leaders, giving them a place to gather and debate and discuss issues. Coffee came to America in the 1700s, and today coffee is the world's most popular beverage. More than 400 billion cups are consumed each year, making coffee second only to oil as the world's largest import—mull *that* over with a grande drip.

SE Portland

Crema is located in the lovely Southeast quadrant of Portland, Oregon. Besides espresso, it features French-press coffee, loose leaf teas, morning pastry, and other cakes and treats. Casey, a barista for about four years, the most recent two here at Crema, talks freely about the difference between coffee cultures in Seattle and Portland and how it seems people in the industry often get too territorial. "We should just come together—after all, we all love coffee." Casey really enjoys working in this neighborhood and fits right in with the overall welcoming atmosphere of the area. He loves making drinks and putting cool art on top.

Crema is known throughout Portland for its delicious baked goods. Mmmmm, cupcakes...

World Famous
ELLIOTT BAY CAFE
↰ *Down Stairs*

LUNCH
COFFEE
PASTRIES

PIONEER SQUARE

FAVORITE PART
OF THE JOB: Free Coffee
ON MUSIC: If we weren't under
a bookstore, I would listen
to KMFDM or Skinny Puppy.
But, since we've got to
keep things kind of quiet, I
like to put on Bauhaus
or Sisters of Mercy.

CHRIS (3-PLUS YEARS)

Overheard in the Coffeehouse

"Awesome night—really awesome. Until I woke up in my own piss. Can I get a quad shot in the dark?"

"My wife's in labor, and we're on our way to the hospital—can I get two grande nonfats really fast?"

Two 20-something girls:

"She said that you—?"
"Yes!"
"No!"
"Yes!"
"No!"
"Yes!"
"No!"
"Yes!"
"Really?"

Unknown male to a female couple:

"Just wanted to let you know that I'd be a sperm donor for you. I've done it before and I heard you talking about stuff."

"Can you turn the Internet on?"

Espresso Express

Ravenna

Espresso Express opened 24 years ago. Carl, the manager, has been here 20 years and Adrianne, our assistant manager, has been here about 16 years now! We are one of the first espresso-based coffee shops in the area, and it all started with a trip to Tahiti. You see, in 1983 I went on a wonderful vacation to Tahiti, where every day for breakfast I

> This building was originally a gas station, and now, too, we offer Dr. Dan's Biodiesel! We've come full circle from gas, to espresso, and now gas again.

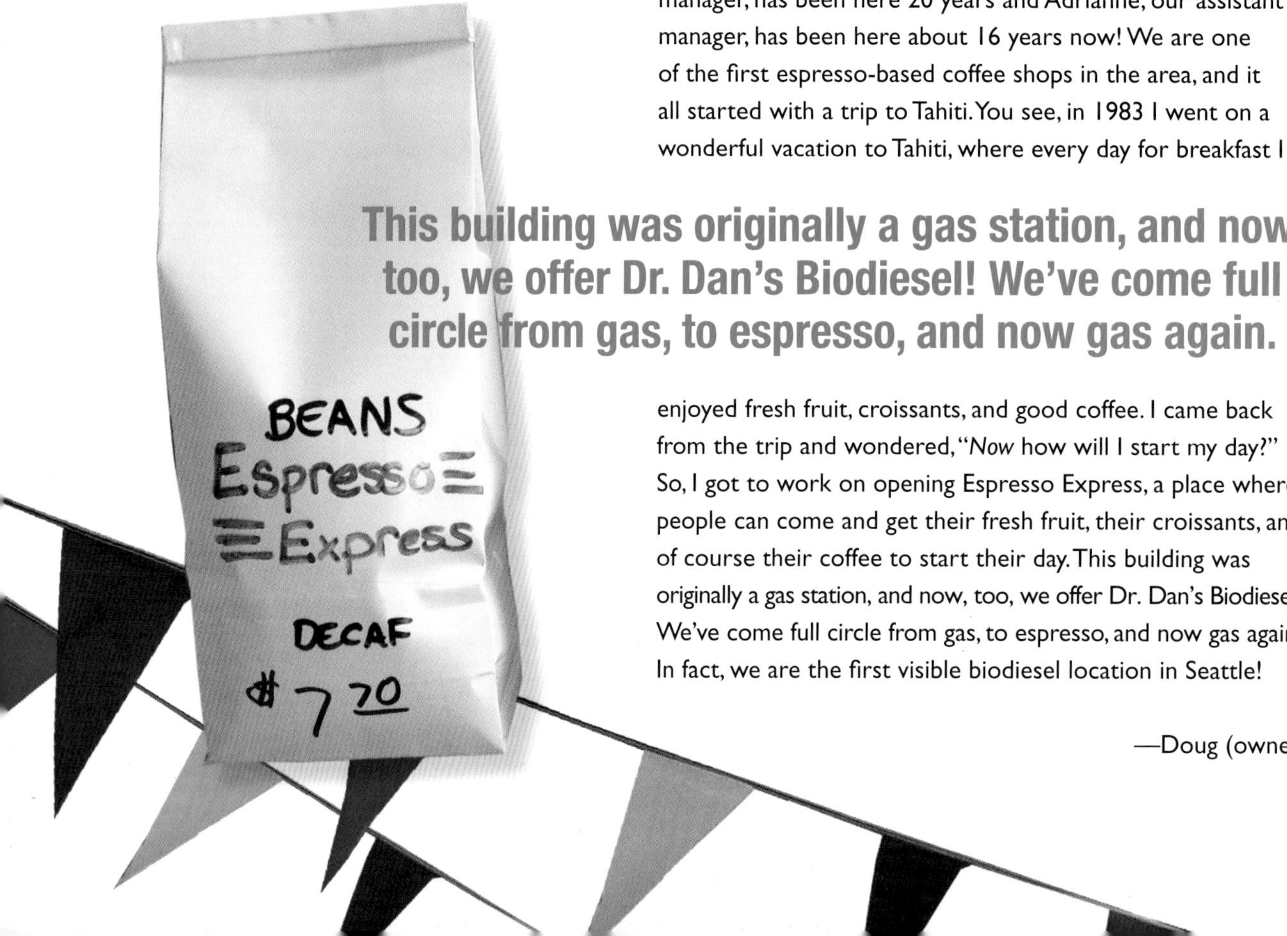

enjoyed fresh fruit, croissants, and good coffee. I came back from the trip and wondered, "*Now* how will I start my day?" So, I got to work on opening Espresso Express, a place where people can come and get their fresh fruit, their croissants, and of course their coffee to start their day. This building was originally a gas station, and now, too, we offer Dr. Dan's Biodiesel! We've come full circle from gas, to espresso, and now gas again. In fact, we are the first visible biodiesel location in Seattle!

—Doug (owner)

BEANS
Espresso
Express

DECAF
$7 70

GRANITAS !

FAST LATTE * PRIMO ..

Now serving espresso
AND biodiesel!

Doug

Vivace

e s p r e s s o

una bella tazza di caffe

Capitol Hill
Denny Regrade

This skill/art saved MY sanity

Christopher "Nicely" Abel Alameda has been a barista for 2 years. Described by his fellow baristas as annoyingly passionate, a welcoming host, naturally gifted, and professional, he exudes all of this and more while pouring his favorite drink: mochas.

Nicely

zach

The chocolate, Nicely says, allows him to play with a lot of color in the cup when pouring the design. A close second? Vivace's Cafe Nico, a 4-oz orange-flavored breve macchiato with an orange zest and cinnamon sprinkled over the top. The most "interesting" drink he's made? A 10-shot, 12-oz sugar-free vanilla nonfat latte.

"I love that my job is the perfect balance between art and skill. We try our best to show you a level of attention in everything we do, including what ends up on the top of your drink. For even just a moment, if you can look at your coffee and see something beautiful, perhaps that will allow room for a happy thought or two. We caffeinate teachers, doctors, lawyers, construction workers, artists, students, people from every walk of life. On a daily basis I know I am helping someone start or make it through the day with a carefully prepared cup of coffee. People that I may otherwise never meet end up becoming loyal customers."

EXTRACTO *Coffeehouse* NE Portland

Marty

Extracto owners Chris and Celeste opened their shop just a couple of years ago, and according to the neighbors, they had a quiet yet loyal start for the first few months. Not so anymore. Nowadays the café is packed with a nonstop line to the door. Though there is just a modest A-board sign outside and no other advertising to be found, people in the area (and elsewhere!) have learned about the pleasures of Extracto and flock to it. Chris and Celeste plan to start roasting.

Marty, a favorite barista (4 years) here, loves to roast coffee at home and will soon be roasting for Extracto.

Jaime, another barista (3 years), enjoys photography, film, salsa, and speaking Spanish.

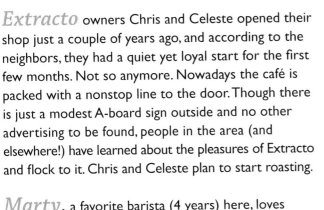

Jaime

Geography of the Bean

Ever wonder how where a bean is grown changes its overall flavor and finish? Mason Sager, a roaster at Caffé Vita, describes the differences between Vita's different blends.

Africa

Caffé Vita Farm Direct Shashamane (Ethiopia): This coffee is from a high-altitude farm (1,800 meters) located 3 kilometers northeast of Yirgacheffe, Ethiopia. A beautiful coffee displaying classic traits of coffees found in the Yirgacheffe region: fragrant, herbaceous aromas of honeysuckle, lemon, and bergamot, balanced with a delicate, light body, moderately bright, with flavors of citrus, honey, and a very subtle hint of dark chocolate in the finish.

Kenya Auction Lot AA: Our Kenyan coffees are sourced from the best of the weekly coffee auctions in Nairobi, Kenya, which consistently provide us with classic, top-shelf coffees throughout the year. Coffee is sourced from the regions of Kiambu, Kirinyaga, Thika, and Machakos on a seasonal basis.

The coffees sourced display the classic features of Kenyan premium coffees, including bright citruslike acidity of lemon and grapefruit with deep herbal undertones and a balance of raisin, dark chocolate, and citrus flavors in the finish.

Central America

Caffé Vita Farm Direct Finca Nuevo Viñas (Guatemala): This coffee is sourced from a Rainforest Alliance–certified coffee farm and displays many characteristics of a classic Guatemalan coffee: aromas of dark chocolate balanced with floral notes of citrus and honeysuckle. This is a medium-bodied, moderately bright coffee with well-balanced flavors of cocoa, citrus, and roasted hazelnuts, with a sweet finish.

Caffé Vita Farm Direct Organic Finca Dos Jefes (Panama): A truly unique, world-class coffee. From the Finca Dos Jefes coffee plantation in Panama, this high-elevation, naturally processed, certified organic coffee displays bold aromas of dark chocolate and blueberry, complemented by moderately bright acidity and a full body.

Organic Mexico Chiapas: This organic coffee is grown outside the village of Motozintla in the mountainous region of Chiapas, Mexico. A wonderfully bright, well-balanced coffee with rich aromatic tones of chocolate, citrus, and baking spice. The chocolate aromas carry through to the cup: medium bodied, balanced with citrus, caramel, and a subtly spicy aftertaste.

South America

Caffé Vita Farm Direct Carmo Nero de Minas (Brazil): This coffee is sourced from the Sul de Minas region in southeastern Brazil. A rich, medium- to full-bodied coffee with intoxicating aromas of chocolate, butterscotch, and citrus. A relatively low-acid coffee with well-balanced flavors of dark chocolate, citrus, and hints of cinnamon in the finish.

Colombia Huila Valencia: This coffee is sourced from the high-elevation southern Colombia region of Huila. Dark chocolate aromas with subtle hints of pear and vanilla. A classic display of grapefruit-like acidity is found in this bright, medium-bodied coffee balanced with dark chocolate, lush vanilla, and a tapering caramel-like finish.

Indonesia

Caffé Vita Farm Direct IKA Organic Sumatra Mandheling: Sourced from the organic IKA coffee farm in the Mandheling region of Sumatra, this coffee displays the classic characteristics of world-class Sumatra: big, bold aromas of chocolate, earth, baking spice, tobacco, and smoke. A full-bodied, low-acid coffee balanced with dark chocolate, earth, spice, and smoke, with a sweet, creamy lingering finish.

Papua New Guinea Peaberry Kimel Estate: Sourced from the Kimel Plantation in the famous Wahgi Valley in the western highlands of Papua New Guinea. Grown at an altitude of more than 1,500 meters, this coffee displays sweet aromas of chocolate, spice, and citrus, balanced with crisp acidity, chocolate, caramel, and citrus with subtle hints of smoke and a clean finish.

FIREHOUSE coffee

No 1

BALLARD

CRYSTAL (5 YEARS). LISTENING TO: RADIOHEAD, LIONEL RICHIE.

FAVES:

HAPPY PEOPLE, MAKING DRY CAPPUCCINOS, GREAT COWORKERS, FREE COFFEE!

LEAST FAVES:

GETTING UP AT 6 A.M. ON THE WEEKENDS, DOING DISHES, LIME LATTES.

We started

with the coffee shop about five years ago, March 2003. My daughter, Anya runs it, and I told her we'd give it two years to make a profit and then we'll see—well, it only took six months! We've got a wonderful community here at Fremont Coffee. We pretty much have the same staff from the day we opened! I started as a traditional, trained herbalist and I love all kinds of herbs: chocolate, teas, coffee, you name it. I love the overall experience of coffee, though. Each coffee has its distinct characteristics, flavors, qualities, properties, and more. Coffee is just a wonderful, living plant. You know, whatever you do, you've got to start out with ambition; where it ends up, who knows, but you've got to start with that.

—Chris Parker, owner

fremont
coffee company
F.C.C.

Great times out on the Porch

THE FRESH POT

an independent cafe

N Portland, Hawthorne District

MORGAN

"I've been a barista for a while, but only for about a year here. This is the only one that counts."

My life is beautiful,

roasted in beautiful portland, oregon

thefreshpot.com

400 n. mississippi & 3729 se. hawthorne

FP

MICHAEL

Michael has been working at the Fresh Pot since it opened its second location (on North Mississippi Avenue) over six years ago. He's been a barista for ten years and absolutely loves it. "At this point, I've seen the same cutomers for over five years here. We know about each other and about each other's lives." Michael also enjoys the culture of the industry as a whole, and keeps up with the latest trends, refinements, and technologies. When he's not managing the shop or busy behind the bar, Michael writes for *Barista Magazine*.

and coffee is my life.

Mr. Stink and the Ice Queen

By Julie Poole, The Fresh Pot, Portland, OR

Nothing could have prepared me for the Ice Queen. Or maybe I was already having one of those days. She was abrupt in a fascinating way, in a way that disregarded the social norms preventing fights from breaking out in the grocery store. She weaved to the front of the line, grabbed various cookies from a plate on the counter, and held one up to me. "What kind of cookie is this?" she asked, ignoring the pretty sign labeled "Chocolate chip, $1.75."

"Chocolate chip," I said, *as indicated by the chocolate chips embedded in the pale dough,* I finished in my head.

"Is it made with butter?" she asked, her East Coast accent replacing the last *r* with an *ah*.

"Yes it is," I replied curtly, smiling at the meek girl in horn-rimmed glasses and a grandma cardigan whose rightful turn it was.

"Because I can't eat margarine."

Turning to the meek girl, I asked, "What would you like to drink today?" and like a sweet little fish, she opened her mouth to speak and clamped it shut again as the Ice Queen squawked, "How much is it?"

"$1.75," I said.

"Expensive," she sniffed. "OK, I'll take this and an iced latte, extra ice."

"Sure," I said. "But the line actually starts down there," I pointed.

"Oh," she huffed.

She set her belongings down on a table: a purse, a smaller purse, and a reusable grocery bag from New Seasons that served as a purse, and after pushing two tables together she emptied the contents of her bags: a laptop, books, cell phone,

notepad, a large bottle of Perrier, and a bag of granola. She put on her narrow jelly-bean-colored reading glasses with a long beaded chain and peered at me as she took her place in line and vigorously coiled her hair into an upsweep, securing it with decorated chopsticks in two violent stabs.

My face grew hot as she approached and flung the cookie like a discus onto the counter. I put the ice into the pint glass and she asked for more. I filled it until the cubes fell out. After I added the milk and shots, she again asked for "more ice." I returned to the ice bucket and mounded every cube that I could possibly fit into the glass until it looked like a snow cone. I slid the glass across the counter with a little too much force, because it spun into her hand. She didn't seem to notice and coolly thanked me.

She returned to her "home office" and began pecking away loudly at her keyboard. The next customer wanted a double shot, which always made me nervous because it's the true test of a barista's skills. He fiddled with his new iPhone and wore expensive workout gear. Probably one of the new condo owners, I thought. He'd clearly just gotten done with a run, because his hair was wet and his well-formed muscles glistened. He took his demitasse cup to the end of the counter and picked through *The New York Times* to find the business section. The Ice Queen eyed him from under her glasses for a while, got up, went over to him, and said something that made his face cringe. He shook his head, and she returned to her seat.

He came over to me and peered over the bar. "Do I smell bad?" he asked. "That woman just told me that I have BO, told me to leave."

Not pleased with my delayed response, he turned to two women who were stirring honey into their coffee. "Do I stink?" he asked them. They shook their heads, and one said,

"I don't smell you," but I thought they might not tell the truth anyway because he clearly looked so hurt.

"That woman was so rude. Will you go over and tell her that I don't have to leave and that she should leave?" he asked.

"I'm sorry sir, I can't tell her to leave," I said.

"But she was rude to me." His voice cracked like a teenager, in a way that made me think people weren't often rude to him. After all, he was a handsome, wealthy, metrosexual-looking man, one who probably had a skin-care regimen.

"So you're not going to say something to her?"

"I'm sorry sir, my hands are tied. Make yourself comfortable and ignore her," I said.

He didn't seem pleased but went to sit at a table far away from where she sat. She was clearly the stronger personality, and when I glanced at her table I noticed that she had one of her headphones off so that she could eavesdrop on our conversation.

My coworker Mike D. came in just then to pick up his paycheck and pour himself a cup of coffee for the road. Mike played rugby, and although he was only 5 foot 8, he had the loping stride of a much larger guy. Working with him was like watching a play-by-play; he'd get stoned and clean everything. I liked him but tried to stay out of his way. He worked a second job as a bouncer at a dance club called Storefront that many of his girl groupies went to. They got a double dose of him at night at the club and in the morning when he made them their hangover coffee. Mike and I bitched a little about work, and I tried to tell him about the customer situation.

I went over to help someone who had just stepped up to the counter and saw Mr. Stink approach Mike, possibly thinking he was the manager. He had the look of someone with authority. Mike listened to his plea and tried to reason with him, explaining that we couldn't kick out the Ice Queen just because she said something rude. The Ice Queen came up to the counter and asked for more ice for her drink and calmly sat down again. She eyed Mr. Stink with amusement. *Some people!* I imagined her saying. Meanwhile the meek girl looked longingly for a place to sit. Not only did the Ice Queen take up two tables, her computer cords were strung across another available seat. Mr. Stink wasn't pleased with Mike's response, and Mike was clearly peeved that he was cornered on his way out the door. Mr. Stink approached the Ice Queen's table nervously and said, "You were rude to me and never in my life—"

"Sir!" interrupted Mike. "Sir, leave her alone."

"But—" Mr. Stink looked confused.

"Now I'm going to have to ask you to leave," Mike said.

"This is ridiculous!" cried Mr. Stink.

By that time everyone's attention was on Mr. Stink, who was so clearly embarrassed and frazzled that he dropped his little cup on the ground. He wiped the sweat from his brow and tucked our *Times* under his arm and left. I felt bad for him, and told Mike how the Ice Queen really was a bitch, forgetting how she still had her one ear uncovered. Mike explained to me that it didn't matter who was right or who was wrong; it was the person escalating the situation who was the problem. That's how he decided who to kick out of the club when there was a bar fight. I considered this, and although I felt bad for Mr. Stink because he'd finally worked up the courage to say something to the Ice Queen, that's just how it goes. By the time you know what to say to defend yourself, it's too late.

CAPITOL HILL
MONTLAKE
WALLINGFORD

GET GOING

SEATTLE

Dani, owner
barista of 17 years

Two Perspectives on Northwest Coffee Culture

Maddie Stevenson

I am a born-and-raised Seattleite, born into coffee privilege. Being white, lower middle class, and having a coffee-drinking barista momma, I pretty much was destined to be a coffee snob. Predisposed and preconditioned. My mom was a barista at the first Starbucks, before it became a corporate monster, seeping into the earth and spreading like morning glory, popping up in the most unexpected places all across the world. This was also before Starbucks switched to automatic machines, before the actual taste of its coffee went to s**t. Before it bastard-ized the trade. Before the coffee war was waged. Back before Seattle disowned its baby.

I became a coffee addict at a young age, living in a city full of self-medicated, overcaffeinated people. However, I didn't really come into my full-blown coffee connoisseur attitude until I left my home-town and ventured cross-country. To my mind the whole nature of an epic road trip requires plenty of caffeine and nicotine. Something besides gas to fuel those long nights on the road, just trying to get from point A to point B. There is some kind of nuance in holding on to the wheel, a cigarette stuck between your index and middle finger, your free hand grasping a hot cup of joe. Just two broke teenage girls, barreling down the dark highway, trying to get as far away from home as possible on a tight budget. It sounds ridiculous, but even if we denied ourselves a bed and instead opted to sleep sitting up in the Volkswagen, we never denied ourselves our daily coffee binge. I will admit that at first we would hooray when we saw a Starbucks on the side of the highway. We knew that we were truly in a foreign place when all we could find was truck-stop automatic; push the button and scorching hot watery Irish cream crap spews out into your Styrofoam cup. We grew to love it though.

So when we finally made our way out of the South-west landscape and back to the coast to settle in San Diego, the coffee there seemed decadent. Shots of espresso—what a concept! My first nesting tendency when moving to a new community is to find my new coffee shop, my new hangout place, meet my new barista. People, as in surfer-bro locals, thought that me and my roommate were strange for haunting that coffee shop, but it was just part of our daily routine, a deeply ingrained tendency to socialize with the background noise of a coffee grinder. We weren't strange; we were Seattle.

I only lasted six months before I had visions of heading back up the coast to Seattle, getting an apartment on Capitol Hill with hardwood floors, watching rain slick the streets, working as a coffee slinger. I still remember the first latte I had when I came home. It was at a coffee shop in Fremont that I was reborn, that the synapses in my brain exploded, that my inner coffee snob was realized. With that first sip of milky espresso delight I realized just how exceptionally high the coffee standards are in this city. Thanks to the constant demand and competition, even remote coffee shops have to be good to get business. I used to think the common thought that "coffee is coffee." But once you get coffee that is so well done you don't want to add sugar, milk, or syrups to it, you begin to rank your coffee experiences, and you begin your quest for the ideal cup.

I had been waitressing in San Diego, and when I left I swore that I was never going to serve or work in a restaurant again. It drained me in so many ways. Not only did I hate the way people treated me and the sexual harassment, but I hated the scene and the culture of waiters and bartenders. I wanted no part of it, but what was I to do with no college degree, only able to work part-time because of my school load? In this service-oriented economy, restaurant work is one of the last decent-paying occupations. I sure as hell wasn't going to get paid minimum wage to work retail. I realized that it was time for me to try to break into the elite Seattle coffee scene.

When I was 15 my mom fell in love in a café. He was the roaster of a well-known coffee supplier at the time, and when they married my coffee status was upped. They eventually moved from Seattle and started their own coffee-roasting business. But his name was still well known, and that was my in: I just slapped it on the bottom of a few résumés and got quite a few calls.

I chose to work at the coffee shop I'm at now specifically because I liked the owner and the vision of the business. The coffee was great, the standards high, but most of all the baristas weren't snobby and intimidating. Customer service was emphasized, which is quite different than the other coffee shops nearby. In most other places the baristas have this self-righteous manner of delivery, and if you ask politely for any sort of modification to your order, they look at you like you're an uncultured tourist who has no idea what good coffee even is.

Being a new barista is intimidating. So many in this city are on the quest for the perfect cup of coffee. I don't think most people realize just how hard it is to get the perfect shot, the perfect temperature, the perfect milk foam, the perfect latte design. It's difficult but true coffee junkies want no less. But the challenge is good, and I love my job. It's like being a drug dealer—people treat you with needy respect. The bar being a barrier helps as well. It really tops being a waitress, and the tips are good. Because customers can watch you work, they see how demanding it is and often are more patient. Conversation between barista and consumer is much more a part of the experience, and you do develop close connections with your regulars. All in all being a coffee snob/barista isn't bad. It's a privileged role I was born into, in a sense, and I can live with that. I don't plan on being in the service industry forever, but being a barista really beats my other options while I am a student. I will, however, probably be a coffee snob for the rest of my life because, after all, I am a Seattleite.

Scott Richardson

The early '90s found me pulling shots at a suburban drive-through while studying at the University of Washington. During my drive-through tenure, I competed in barista competitions driven by syrups rather than coffee (it was a different era). It was at that company that the roasting carrot was dangled before me. Although roasting never worked out at that gig, it began my research and passion for coffee. From there I took jobs selling and servicing espresso equipment and coffee brewers, roasting coffee on a large scale for a growing Seattle-based roaster, then providing tech support nationwide for yet more coffee equipment before landing at Herkimer Coffee. Throughout that entire time, I experimented with, researched, messed up, and dialed in just about anything coffee-related I could think of. Looking back, I started coffee while in art school; I guess that worked out pretty well.

How did coffee get so big in Seattle? Lots of reasons come to mind. Seattle's weather would be the one most people, especially those involved in the industry, can agree on. More importantly, I think coffee got to where it is today by growing out of an independent spirit attached to a value of aesthetics. The independent spirit comes from our geographical isolation from the rest of the country and the aesthetics from the abundant natural beauty found in our region.

The first specialty-coffee purveyors here sought out the techniques used by the Italians to introduce espresso, cappuccino, and the mystery of the coffee-house experience. People enjoyed the personalization that individually prepared drinks offered. Since then the shop owners, roasters, and baristas have constantly raised the bar for themselves and their competition by researching and experimenting with whatever aspect of coffee they enjoyed most. Baristas are constantly honing their skills to compete in latte art and barista competitions. Roasters travel the tropics in search of special single-origin coffee and great producers to establish direct and unique trade systems. Everybody does it just a bit differently from everybody else, which gives people the option to choose their favorites. I think this variety, independent spirit, and aesthetic appreciation are what has fueled our large and diverse coffee culture as it has developed over the last 30 years.

HERKIMER ★ COFFEE

Phinney Ridge, University District

It has been a very long road from "Get the *#!@ out of my drive-thru" to "Hi, I am the manager, what can I do for you?" I started pulling coffee at a drive-through in 1993 and worked my way up the ladder to becoming a manager at Herkimer Coffee in 2003 and running the two cafés since. I turned something I really enjoyed drinking into a full blown career. Each day I learn something new and have new experiences while also getting to teach people how to do the same—which isn't easy, but I love a good challenge! Herkimer is a great environment where we all get to be ourselves while purveying a really great coffee that we are all proud of and love. I finally got to a place I can call home, and there are very few days that I don't want to come to work. That is what life as a career barista should be about: loving what you do and having the flexibility to do other things too. Getting up at 4:30 a.m. is tough, but not when you get off at noon!

—Kara MacDonald, retail manager

Kara

"NEXT?"
"CAN I GET A.
GRANDE CARAMEL
MACCHIATO?"

AMAZING!

Katy & Tim

PLAYLIST=
• KEXP 90.3 fm
• ANY AMBIANT JAZZ
• ANY LOOP RECORD
  (New Zealand labels)
• ANY NEW ZEALAND
  MUSIC / HIP HOP

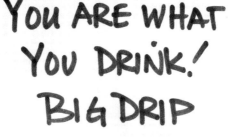

YOU ARE WHAT
YOU DRINK!
BIG DRIP

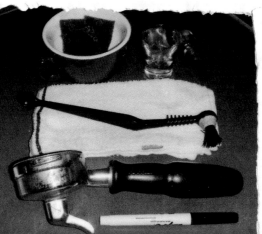

"CAN I JUST GET
  A.....
QUAD GRANDE
NON FAT SPLIT·SHOT
SUGER FREE VANILLA
  LATTE?"

Irwin's

Neighborhood Bakery & Coffee House

Wallingford

Linda

Salads Bagels

Blueberry Muffin

Pumpkin-Walnut Muffin

Located on a corner in the bustling Wallingford neighborhood, Irwin's opened its doors over ten years ago as a neighborhood bakery and coffee house. Locals flock to the shop for their daily coffee, fresh baked goods, and familiar faces. After years of working behind the scenes doing the books for Irwin's, Linda, the current owner, got her opportunity to step up front and take the reins. "It was like that little-girl dream you have that you never say out loud for fear of ruining its chances of coming true. It was a perfect match—the [previous] owner was thinking of moving on and I wanted nothing more than to move in! She had such a good thing going with the culture she created here and the real community feel, and I loved every part of it." Linda, a single mother of three teenagers, acquired Irwin's in August 2006 and has since split her time between working the bar three days a week, baking three days a week, and now delivering her baked goods to wholesale customers during the wee hours too. "More and more I am just loving the bakery. Number one for me is always the customers; I love this neighborhood and I love the people and our place in this community. I got into this business for the people and the coffee, but now the bakery, too, is really growing a special place in my heart." Linda's mission statement is simple, strong, and straightforward: "A single woman who owns a business has to have her complete heart and soul in it in order to make it." Linda herself is a perfect example of just that.

Ballard, West Seattle

Tony, the owner

Tony started Java Bean as a cart in Seattle in 1989, when there were maybe only half a dozen carts in the area. As the demand for, and knowledge of, a "café culture" grew, Java Bean's cart evolved into Java Bean coffee shops in three prominent Seattle neighborhoods: Ballard, Greenwood, and West Seattle. His favorite part of the job is making coffee for people who have never had gourmet, craftsman-style coffee, people who can really enjoy the educational aspect of the process and the product. His best advice: "Be a craftsman and love the true craft of coffee."

Ryan loves her job. Her interests include music, art, fashion, going to local shows: "Seattle is great for that!" Words of wisdom for newbies: "Don't be afraid to ask questions! Ask experienced baristas and your customers for advice and insight, even if you've been doing this for a while."

Jonathan is a people person, perfectionist, hard worker, and congenial. "I get to talk to cool people, get free coffee, make latte art—there's always something to improve upon. If I wasn't a barista, I'd be writing poetry and short stories, and taking photos every day."

Ryan,
(1 year)

Jonathan,
(4-plus years)

Coffee Shop

Patty Jahn, the owner of Java Jahn, has been serving espresso in the neighborhood for over 17 years. The first 12 of those years were spent outside a hardware store with an espresso cart, and her business built from there. Five years ago she bought the building across the street from where she'd run the cart and moved the operation inside, providing her customers with a warm and welcoming place to get their coffee, pastries, conversation, news, and more. Patty Jahn is well-respected, well-loved, and definitely a notable part of the community.

joe bar

COFFEE

CAPITOL HILL

WYLIE, OWNER

ADVICE FOR A NEW BARISTA?
Stay calm. Let it go.

IS THERE A SPECIFIC WAY PEOPLE SHOULD ORDER DRINKS?
Efficiently and NOT in a whisper.

La résistance est futile.

WHAT IS YOUR FAVORITE/LEAST FAVORITE PART OF THE JOB?
Favorite: the odd conversation.
Least: the odd conversation.

JOBS PERKS/HAZARDS?
Perks: free coffee.
Hazards: hot water burns.

WHAT FEW WORDS DESCRIBE YOU AS A BARISTA?
Friendly and often interested.

IF YOU WEREN'T A BARISTA, WHAT
WOULD YOU BE DOING?
Interior design.

—Sarah (3½ years)

BRYNNA

Ask Dani

Q. *Dani, what's the best way to pick up a barista?*

A. Some suggestions:
- Use both hands and bend at the knees.
- Tip well.
- Be polite. Manners go further than attempted wit.
- Don't ask him or her out for coffee.
- Order a double short americano. Or a macchiato. Show your barista that you appreciate the bean.

Q. *How can I tell if my barista is flirting back at me?*

A. She or he is not. Don't mistake good customer service for flirting. But if your barista seems to be really forward, and you think you may have a chance, see my response to the above question. And count yourself lucky. Go ahead and order a triple short latte.

Q. *My boyfriend is good looking and well dressed—and he just told me he wants to be a barista. Is he gay?*

A. Not necessarily. Baristas, like ordinary people, come in all shapes, sizes, ages, races, religions, musical genres, and sexual orientations. Though he'll soon be entering an exciting world of caffeine-induced beauty, drama, adventure, trysts, and other reality-show components, you shouldn't be worried. If your relationship is shaky and/or you have security issues, only then should you take some time to rethink your situation. Call me. We'll talk it out over split-shot americanos.

Q. *My girlfriend has been getting more tattoos and made really good tips today. Should I be worried?*

A. Yes. She's ours now. Try to hang on and do something extra thoughtful, like buy her an engraved tamp in her favorite color/material. Splurge and order a frilly drink, like a vanilla-caramel mocha with whip—it might make you feel better. But if she asks what you're drinking, deny it and say it's something more respectable, like a capp.

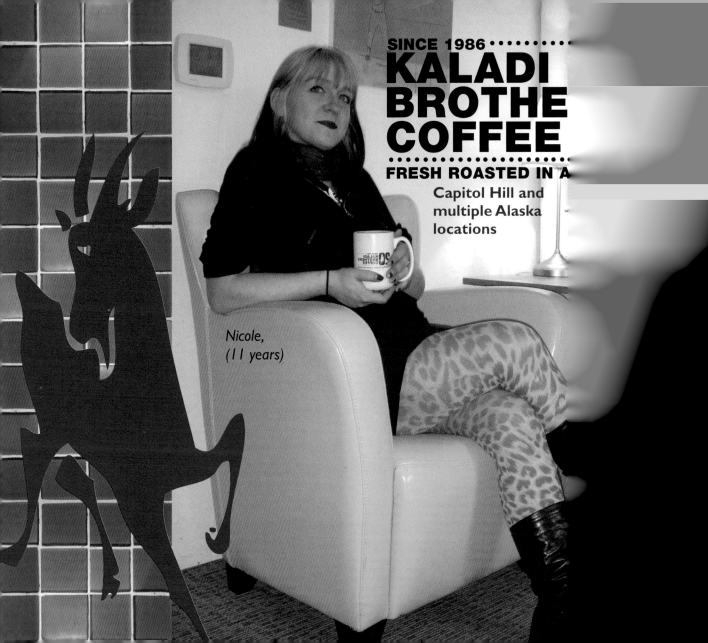

SINCE 1986 •••••••••

KALADI
BROTHE
COFFEE

FRESH ROASTED IN A

Capitol Hill and
multiple Alaska
locations

Nicole,
(11 years)

I've been a barista since I was 16, starting out at a super-busy shop in Tacoma, since then I've basically gone from shop to shop to shop; being a barista is just the greatest job, especially for me since I'm energetic and outgoing and pretty much a social butterfly and I love to talk to people, have regular customers, work with great people, and just get to be fabulous; one of the most memorable drinks I've made was a 6 shot, rice milk, mint-raspberry mocha—yuck! do you even like coffee?!—and when people order their drinks, I think what's more important than the order of specifics (tall, double, kind of milk, etc.) is that they order nice and slow so the barista can understand … some people are in such a hurry! :) to be a good waitress you have to be a good diner, the same is true in coffee: to be a good barista, you have to be a good coffee customer.

Oh Cascade,
When did you
become South
lake Union?

Doug Peterson

"It's just Jeremiah and I who run the shop. I put one ad in one paper when I opened 10 years ago looking for a barista. Jeremiah answered the ad and has stayed ever since!"

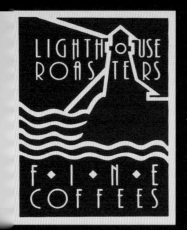

LIGHTHOUSE ROASTERS

F·I·N·E COFFEES

FREMONT

Jon, 8 years, listens to Poison, Billy Joel, Simon and Garfunkel and starts out every morning with Journey's "Don't Stop Believin'"

What few words describe you as a barista? Late.

Hobbies/interests? Fantasy football, Guitar Hero

Job perks/hazards? Mariner's tix

Favorite drink to make? Double short americano

Why is this the best job ever? Off @ 1:00 pm

WILSON

JON

JOHN

PETER

DON'T STOP BELIEVIN'

A Field Guide to Items Found in a Coffee Shop

Aprons: Though previously shunned as a symbol of corporate control measures, the apron is trying to make a comeback! It definitely helps to stave off coffee-stained clothing and serves as a handy barrier between the barista and accidentally overflowing steamed milk. Some say it even adds a bit of professionalism to our often-overlooked career!

Bar towel: A staple behind the bar. Plenty are on hand for portafilters, counters, tables, and the occasional barista rag-snap-fight (akin to, but way more sophisticated than, the locker-room towel-snap scenarios).

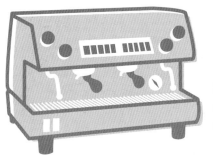

Espresso machine: No room for compromise here. Seek out a café with a good one.

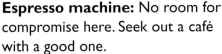

"Extra Love" button: A mythical button on a cash register that supposedly adds a small surcharge for those "extra special" customers.

Nail scrubber/industrial soap/lotion: Bleach dries out hands. Coffee stains hands—and everything else. Seriously, between the calluses and the coffee stains, baristas probably won't be hand models.

Outlets: Coffee shop campers' best friends. Is your office a café? Then you know what I'm talking about!

Pitchers: For steaming milk. Whether specially crafted for latte art or to meet milk-steaming standards, the pitcher is an essential tool in specialty coffee preparation.

Portafilter: Attaches to the group head of espresso machines and carries a tamped puck of coffee grounds within its basket. It is usually made of brass and is attached by a plastic or wooden handle. The portafilter forms a seal with the espresso machine's gasket and directs high-pressure hot water through the coffee puck. Aftermarket retailers also sell bottomless portafilters that minimize the espresso's contact with any metal. A bottomless portafilter is one tool baristas use to analyze the quality of the coffee grind and the evenness of the extraction.

Tamp(er): The all-important barista tool. After the espresso beans are ground, they are pulled into the portafilter and then tamped with just the right amount of pressure to pack the grounds evenly and ensure a perfect pour. Tamps come in many variations, styles, colors, and weights to complement both fashion and function.

Tip jar: Show the love here. Baristas are personally tailoring and crafting your perfect drink. And making minimum wage.

Local Color

Art. Coffee.
& More...

Sydne B. Albanese
Principal/Resident Artist

1606 Pike Place Seattle, WA 98101   Tel. 206.728.1717
sydne@LocalColorSeattle.com   www.LocalColorSeattle.com

LISTENING TO: CLASSICAL MUSIC

*F*rank and Sydne opened Local Color right in the heart of the famous Pike Place Market in July 2003. The shop offers "coffee, art, and more" and is filled with just that, including resident artist Sydne's art studio right on site. Frank says "We just love the people in the market. You truly get to meet all types from total transients to Bill Gates and everyone in between. The best is how flocks of tourists come all the time, and they always ask the vendors in the market how to get to the original Starbucks, where's the original Starbucks, etc. Everyone tells them go down a block, get your picture with the sign, then turn around and go to Local Color for coffee!"

When not pouring his favorite drink to make, a dry cappuccino, Frank's [and Sydne's] passion is their Harley-Davidson. "We go on road trips whenever possible. In the summer there is a group of riders who meet right here at the shop for some coffee before we head out on the road for the day. It's really something as we turn the Market upside down for about an hour! To all patrons, you're welcome to ride with us!"

Meet them at Local Color, get a coffee, enjoy the art, and then fire it up.

SYDNE AND FRANK

The Lyons' Den
Bothell, WA

THE Lyons' Den

Inside cup: Alex, Tim, Aprille.
Holding giant coffee cup: Brady

morning shift: Morning workers are the Navy Seals of the barista world. Not only do we have the most customers—droves of underslept, uncaffeinated customers who are regular enough to rip you a new one if you forget that their ristretto, half-caf, nonfat, half-vanilla, half-caramel latte comes with whip—but we have to prep and stock everything for the rest of the day. One thing a newbie MUST learn: We tear through setup at lightening speed IN SILENCE!!! Seriously, new barista guy—I don't care about your late-night escapades when it's 5 a.m.!! Just put the stinkin' muffins in the case! I know it's your first day, but can the questions wait until 6!? One more word, Chatty Cathy, and you're going to be kicked off the A team and put on closing shift.

mid shift: Dear God, not another panini.

closing shift: Lucky: The band is good. Luckier: The emo-kid fanbase will show up and leave promptly. Luckiest: Once the panini grill gets cleaned, no one will order a sandwich, and everyone will kindly remember to flush the urinal after using. This is the Closer's reality. Even so, there are things that save us from going postal:

- The blaring music that we dance to while doing the final mopping.
- The most unbelievably tone-deaf rendition of "O Holy Night" played to inform residual customers that we are beyond ready to shut down.
- The way that somehow between the "Do you want to clean the panini tonight?" and the "Turn off the sign—quick before someone comes!" we manage to get everything done.

— Aprille, Brady, Lynn

Tips to Making the Perfect Cup

Adjusting Grind
- Grind espresso per individual serving; adjust by moving the grind a few notches at a time.
- A fine grind will slow shots down; a coarse grind will speed up shots.

Tamping
- Use a dry towel to clean out the portafilter each time.
- Measure coffee dose into the portafilter, and divot remaining grounds into the doser to maintain an even amount of espresso.
- Tamp as evenly and flat as possible using 30 pounds of pressure.
- Keep arm at a 90-degree angle to maintain an even level of grounds and to prevent wrist injury.
- Remove excess grounds from the portafilter.
- Burp machine before placing the portafilter.
- Always keep the portafilter in the group head so it remains hot.

Espresso Extraction
- Extraction should take 22–26 seconds.
- Shots should start as a slow drip and ease into the thickness of angel hair pasta.
- Crema should be thick and caramel colored.
- Shots pulled should fill just below the line on the shot glass.
- For espressos and macchiatos, shots should be pulled as half shots.
- Time your drink preparation so shots can be used immediately.
- Shots should never sit for more than a few seconds.

Milk Steaming
- Always steam per individual servings. Never reheat.
- Milk should be steamed to create a creamy, velvety texture. Introduce air to milk first while the milk is cold. Vary the amount of air into milk depending on how much is being steamed: More air is needed for higher milk volume. Air can only be introduced until milk is lukewarm.

- After adding sufficient air, turn the pitcher to the side and find the spot where milk swirls and sucks up excess bubbles. This produces the creamy foam texture.
- Tamp out bubbles in the milk and swirl it around to get the right consistency.
- Note the different types of milk. Nonfat will expand faster and produce more foam, so less air is needed in the beginning.
- Never let milk sit, as foam will separate (except for cappuccino).
- Know when to use a large pitcher versus a small pitcher for size of cup; the wrong-size pitcher will have less-than-desirable results.
- Monitor milk temperature with hands until it is uncomfortable to the touch, about 140 degrees. Milk loses flavor when it is too hot.
- For cappuccinos, introduce air the whole time (slowly) to get the proper, thick foam.

Drink Preparation
- Get cold milk ready first, then pull shots, and start steaming while shots are being extracted.
- The order of pouring into a cup should be as follows: syrup, shots, and then milk. Espresso is always put into the cup before the milk (except for an americano).

Presentation
- In order to pour the proper design, the consistency of the milk is very important.
- Once you learn proper steaming techniques and extraction, pouring latte art becomes second nature.

Chuck

MMM

monorail
espresso Downtown

On December 1, 1980, Chuck opened Monorail Espresso by Westlake Center in downtown Seattle—under the monorail, of course. His was not only the very first espresso cart in Seattle, but he owned the first espresso cart in the world! The cart, which was made as an experiment, has been Chuck's livelihood and love for the past 27 years and still going strong. After five or so years as a flight attendant, Chuck decided he was ready for a job change. When he wasn't in the air, he and his wife enjoyed biking around Seattle and hanging out at one of this city's first coffee shops in the University District. This got him thinking about opening his own espresso bar (an inside café, not a cart) and he spent some time scouting out good locations. But one fateful day as he was on his way to the dentist for a root canal, he stopped to chat with the gentleman who was experimenting with that original cart. The conversation was exciting and inspiring enough that on the way back from his appointment, Chuck bought the cart operation and jumped right in. "The fact that it's a cash-based business was appealing. One café owner tempted me by fanning a stack of ones in front me—now we can fan twenties!" Chuck is at the forefront of the cart and coffee business in Seattle. He's seen it all, from his original location under the monorail to his current spot on Pike Street, where the cart has been stationed inside for the past 12 years. Chuck loves his business and he loves his free time. When he's not baking cookies for Monorail, he enjoys biking, reading, and life on Bainbridge Island. His current goal? "To come to work and go home on the same ferry!" Monorail Espresso is not only a Seattle icon, but a true groundbreaking institution that paved the way for Seattle's claim to coffee fame.

Serving Double Shots in Seattle Since

1980

MOTORE
COFFEE

DOWNTOWN SEATTLE

Scott, a barista since Motore opened in May of '05, is descbribed as unpredictable and classy. Some of his favorite parts of his job include serving regular customers, making triple tall lattes, drinking free coffee, and his boss.

Scott says BOO to 20-oz dry cappuccinos and a lack of health care. His best advice? "Try to be efficient before you become excellent."

Online
COMPANY

Kyle from the Olive Way Capitol Hill location, a barista of about 6 years, listens to John Coltrane. He says, "The pluses working here are free coffee, good customers, and a 'grande latte for here.' The minuses are too much free coffee, bad customers, eggnog or soy chai tea." His advice for new baristas: "Be patient. This job is great because it's pretty chill."

Capitol Hill, Downtown

Carri &
Dana

Alki Beach

Sleepless Coffee was founded seven years ago in Seattle as a wholesale roaster with distribution throughout the Northwest, California, Arizona, and Nevada. Carri, the president and founder, not only has a background in coffee sales, distribution, and coffee roasting, but also a love of and keen eye for concept, branding, and design. "Our name clearly represents Seattle, the 'coffee capital of the world,' and alludes to caffeine as well." The packaging colors and design, she says, were chosen to represent the company's overall characteristics of being strong, fun, and energetic. Each of the seven blends, three espressos, and five varietals has its own name and marketing piece. Diana, the roastmaster, green coffee buyer, and production manager has been with Sleepless Coffee just over a year now and has an extensive background in the field. Sleepless Coffee also has a highly visible drive-thru location in West Seattle, right on the way to the popular Alki Beach area.

STUMPTOWN COFFEE ROASTERS Portland + Seattle

There is nothing terribly extraordinary about my career in coffee. The things I feel are the most extraordinary are the people I have come to know and work with, and that I am fortunate enough to work for the company I do. The coffee industry in the Pacific Northwest is becoming so refined now that I'm willing to bet if you walk into a coffee roasting company or a café, you will find someone with the title "espresso trainer."

Oftentimes, people entering this industry look to the "espresso trainer" as more of a "master barista," which I think is unfortunate, because they then expect the "master" to wave some sort of wand and bless them with good coffee. Nothing, and especially good coffee, is that easy, and I think it's a nice thought that to get a good cup of coffee, we all have to work with one another. Farmers have to work to sell their coffee, green coffee buyers have to work to find farmers, roasters have to allow the coffee to show its best qualities, and the baristas have to be thoughtful of them all while adjusting their grind. I don't see any masters in that equation, just a bunch of hardworking people.

Customers come in and out every day and expect one thing: good coffee. Some customers may expect a little more, but in the end it is a barista's job to play steward to good coffee, whether explaining where the coffee comes from or pouring latte art on top of chocolate syrup.

—Kyle, barista for 7 years

Capitol Hill
Downtown
Wedgewood

Kim

Christine

Morning staff Kim, a barista of 12 years, and Christine, a barista of 6 years, agree that the best part of the job is the fast pace of work and meeting people. On a typical Sunday morning at 7 a.m., the Capitol Hill shop they work at is quiet with soft, ambient music playing. Then, in just 10 minutes, the entire neighborhood seems to wake up and the place is busy. People come from all over for their morning coffee and, of course, fresh doughnuts to go.

Coffee is much more than a beverage. A coffeehouse is more than just a place to get coffee. Over the past 10 years coffeehouse culture has been turned into the "hurry-up-and-get-'em-out-the-door" culture. We are trying to change that way of thinking. Tougo Coffee Co. encourages you to "stop and smell the coffee." Coffee culture is a way of life for us, and we embrace the diversity within our community, bringing together the people of the TT Minor/Squire Park neighborhoods and Seattle at large.

There is no such thing as a bad customer, only a customer who hasn't had coffee yet.

—Brian Wells, owner

tougo coffee co.

Central District

tougo coffee co.

2007

trabant coffee & Chai Lounge

University District and Pioneer Square

Job Perks: I'm not stuck in a cubicle or office! I love the rush of a rush—multitasking to the max. I get to interact with people all day long, and probably know thousands of people by name—sometimes I feel like a mini-celebrity! There is something romantic and fulfilling about preparing a drink for someone from scratch, which nourishes and comforts them. I have the opportunity to create community among my staff and among my customers. From my little corner of the universe, I can fight the breakneck pace of this world where people drive from home to work to Wal-Mart and don't see a single familiar face the whole day.

Playlist: Los Van Van (Cuba), Bole 2 Harlem (Ethiopia), *Bombay the Hard Way* (Bollywood club remixes)

Best Day: When people are excited about coffee: the process from seed to cup, nuances from different regions, individual palettes, sharing knowledge of coffee-growing and even the particular farm where their coffee came from.

Worst Day: Floods, thefts, robberies—even a truck running into the building. At this point, those things are just funny!

How to Order: Don't worry about the lingo, it was made up in a boardroom. Some of our customers order their favorite latte art on their drinks, like one guy who orders a heart on his cappuccino—except when his ex-wife is in town. Those days he orders a skull.

Stereotypes: *Being a barista is like working fast food.* False! Though there are now super-automatic machines that can turn making a latte into pushing a button, making great coffee is an artisan skill. The craft involves adjusting the grind, dosing, leveling, tamping, consistency, and juggling many factors (temperature, weather, etc.) that each affect the flavor of your shots throughout the day.

Favorite Barista Tool: A tamper is to a barista as a knife is to a chef. Your tamper should fit your body and your personality; we have a shelf of tampers, each with its own name and hand-decorated cozy.

Top 5 Work Albums

1. *Loveless* by My Bloody Valentine
2. *Tender Buttons* by Broadcast
3. *The Smiths* by the Smiths
4. *Stratosphere* by Duster
5. *Daydream Nation* by Sonic Youth

Top 5 Things Customers Say That Make Baristas Want to Punch Them in the Face

1. Happy Friday!!!
2. Why are you yawning? Don't you know you work in a coffee shop?
3. *Barista:* How's it going?
   Customer: Tall mocha.
4. Can I have a caramel macchiato?
5. Really? This is all you do? I assumed you did something else with your free time.

Top 5 Perks of Being a Barista

1. Free coffee
2. Tips
3. Getting to say "I'm a barista"
4. Making connections
5. Making connections with someone you find attractive

—Anonymous barista

Orion, how would you describe
yourself as a barista?
I'm engaging and a little hardheaded.

What is your advice for a new barista?
*The people you serve will become interested
in you as a person if you do them the
same honor.*

If your weren't a barista, what would you be doing?
*Something social, whether it was bartending or
serving. It's become a large part of my life.*

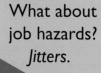

UPTOWN
ESPRESSO

Is there a specific
way people should
order drinks?
With brevity.

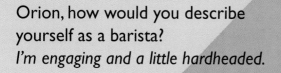

ORION IS
LISTENING TO
JONATHAN RICHMAN
AND THE MODERN LOVERS

What about
job hazards?
Jitters.

VÉRITÉ
COFFEE

Ballard, Madrona, West Seattle

Dear Anchor Tattoo,

I think you're dreamy. you mayBe wanna get a cup of cofFee some time? BUt like, whatever I totalLy doN't even cAre. i'M probably busy that daY. Yeah, i'm totally busy i Think.

♡ Vérité Coffee

Name: Wendy Vollmer
Years as a barista: 2
Favorite drink to make:
doppio macchiato
Favorite drink to drink:
americano
Tattoos by Curtis:
coffee cup, winged skull

Name: Tessa Smith
Years as a barista: 5
Favorite drink to make:
wet cappuccino
Favorite drink to drink:
soy mezzo
Tattoos by Curtis:
foxglove

Name: Rebecca Johnston
Years as a barista: 3
Favorite drink to make:
cappuccino
Favorite drink to drink:
soy macchiato
Tattoos by Curtis:
protea flower

Dear **Vérité** Coffee,

You ha**d** me at hello. I mean, You
comp lete me**?** I mean, yeah ok.
Big whoop. I think Your baristas are
the tatt**o**oiest.

Anchor Tattoo

e: **Curtis James**
s as a tattoo artist: 9
ite tattoo he's done: dog and a bunny
eir haunches. Bunny has his arm around
ays "Best friends 'til the end."
ite tattoo on his body: nurse on
bicep who is crying tears of blood.
te drink: double soy vanilla
om Vérité Coffee!

VICTROLA COFFEE

Capitol Hill

The 15th avenue café is all about community and seriously beautiful coffee. Stop on by for a gorgeously prepared coffee drink, an artisan pastry, a house-made sandwich, or a fancy dessert. Settle in with a good book or some friends to talk to, or just hang out, and you will surely get to know your neighbor and the great staff behind the bar. The new Pike Street location, an old 1920s auto row building just at the border of downtown and Capitol Hill, is where Victrola gets to show off its coffee and roasting operation. You can park yourself at a seat with a view into the roastery or hang out at the window bar and watch the world go by. There is beer and wine too, if you want to mellow out your coffee buzz or just chill out in the late afternoon.

seriously beautiful coffee

Overheard at the Coffeehouse

"Do you have any idea how much money I make?"

Customer to barista:

"Do you guys have any milk back there?"

"He just went running off after the show! We couldn't find him all night, and then he finally showed up this morning wearing hospital scrubs and fell asleep in a f**king tree! F**king Vegas."

One student to another:

"That's good—what site did you buy this [essay] from? Did you see if they have one on intro psych stuff?"

"Yeah, but I don't know if it was ever *really* proven that the world isn't flat."

ZOKA · COFFEE · ROASTER · & · TEA · COMPANY

Greenlake, University District, Snoqualmie

Zoka was opened in 1996 by Jeff Babcock and Tim McCormack in the Greenlake neighborhood of Seattle. Zoka's small-batch roasting, homemade baked goods, hand-picked teas, and of course free Wi-Fi make this cafe a busy and vibrant scene. Zoka is as much dedicated to fine coffee as it is to the community, and so decided to open a second location in the University District, creating yet another neighborhood hot spot and a consistently full house. Zoka invites you to settle in for a while, enjoy the offerings and the atmosphere, and take your time. Coworkers and customers alike are treated like family, and both cafes offer similar scenes: students and neighbors mingling, relaxing, working, studying, talking, and overall enjoying the welcoming atmosphere.

Coffeehouses Featured in this Book

The Albina Press
4637 N Albina Avenue
& 5012 SE Hawthorne Boulevard
Portland, Oregon
Contributors: Kevin, Ben, Billy, Nicole

All City Coffee
1205 S Vale Street
& 125 Prefontaine Place S
Seattle, Washington
www.allcitycoffee.com
Contributors: Seth and Paige

B & O Espresso
204 Belmont Avenue E.
& 416 Broadway E
Seattle, Washington
Contributor: Aleah

Batdorf & Bronson
516 S. Capitol Way
Olympia, Washington
www.dancinggoats.com
Contributors: Jen, Oliver, Michael, Van, and Sasha

Bauhaus Books + Coffee
301 E. Pine Street
Seattle, Washington
Contributors: Grace and Tyler

Bird on a Wire Espresso
3509 SW Henderson Street
West Seattle, Washington
www.birdonawireespresso.com
Contributor: Heidi

Bus Stop Espresso
800 NE 65th Street
Seattle, Washington
Contributors: Levi and Bridget

Cafe Pettirosso
1101 E Pike Street
Seattle, Washington
Contributors: Robin, Yuki, and Danell

Caffé Appassionato
4518 University Way NE
Seattle, Washington
www.caffeappassionato.com
Contributors: Gary and Lauren

Caffé Fioré
5405 Leary Avenue NW, 224 W. Galer Street
& 3125 NW 85th Street
Seattle, Washington
www.caffefiore.com
Contributors: Deming, Joseph, and Linnea

Caffé Ladro
13 locations in the Seattle area
www.caffeladro.com
Contributors: Jack, Sarah, Kevin, Desiree, and David

Caffé Umbria
320 Occidental Avenue S
Seattle, Washington
303 NW 12th Avenue
Portland, Oregon
www.caffeumbria.com
Contributors: Kaci and Jake

Caffé Vita
1005 E Pike Street, 813 5th Avenue N,
4301 Fremont Avenue N & 5028 Wilson Avenue S
Seattle, Washington
124 4th Avenue E.
Olympia, Washington
www.caffevita.com
Contributors: Tom, Daniel, and Mason

Cloud City Coffee
8801 Roosevelt Way NE
Seattle, Washington
www.cloudcitycoffee.com
Contributors: Brooke and Haley

Crema Coffee + Bakery
2728 SE Ankeny Street
Portland, Oregon
www.cremabakery.com
Contributors: Collin and Casey

Elliott Bay Cafe
101 S Main Street
Seattle, Washington
www.elliottbaybook.com
Contributor: Chris

Espresso Express
6500 NE 65th Street
Seattle, Washington
Contributor: Doug

Espresso Vivace
227 Yale Avenue N, 530 Broadway Avenue E
& 321 Broadway Avenue E
Seattle, Washington
www.espressovivace.com
Contributors: David, Nicely, and Zach

Extracto
2921 NE Killingsworth Street
Portland, Oregon
http://extractocoffeehouse.com
Contributors: Chris, Celeste, Marty, and Jaime

Firehouse Coffee
2622 NW Market Street
& 2005 NW Market Street
Seattle, Washington
Contributor: Crystal

Fremont Coffee Company (F.C.C.)
459 N 36th Street
Seattle, Washington
www.fremontcoffee.net
Contributors: Chris, Parker, and Corinne

The Fresh Pot
4001 N Mississippi Avenue
& 3729 SE Hawthorne Boulevard
Portland, Oregon
www.thefreshpot.com
Contributors: Matthew, Michael, Morgan, and Julie

Fuel Coffee
610 19th Avenue E, 2300 24th Avenue E.,
& 1705 N 45th Street
Seattle, Washington
www.fuelcoffeeseattle.com
Contributors: Dani, Maddie, and Rebecca

Herkimer Coffee
7320 Greenwood Avenue N
& 5611 University Way NE
Seattle, Washington
www.herkimercoffee.com
Contributors: Kara, Mike, Katy, and Tim

Irwin's
2123 N 40th Street
Seattle, Washington
Contributor: Linda

Java Bean
5819 24th Avenue NW & 2920 Avalon Way SW
Seattle, Washington
www.javabeancoffee.com
Contributors: Tony, Jonathan, and Ryan

Java Jahn
1428 NW Leary Way
Seattle, Washington
www.javajahn.com
Contributors: Patty and Tanya

Joe Bar
810 E Roy Street
Seattle, Washington
www.joebar.org
Contributors: Wylie, Brynna, and Sarah

Kaladi Brothers Coffee
511 E Pike Street
Seattle, Washington
11 locations in Alaska
www.kaladi.com
Contributor: Nicole

Kapow! Coffee
New location unknown at press time
Seattle, Washington
www.kapowcoffeeshop.com
Contributor: Angela

Lighthouse Roasters
400 N 43rd Street
Seattle, Washington
www.lighthouseroasters.com
Contributors: Jon, John, Jeff, Phil, Peter, and Wilson

Local Color
1606 Pike Place
Seattle, Washington
www.localcolorseattle.com
Contributors: Frank and Sydne

The Lyons' Den
10415 Beardslee Boulevard
Bothell, Washington
www.myspace.com/thelyonsden
Contributors: Lynne, Aprille, Brady, Alex, and Tim

Monorail Espresso
520 Pike Street
Seattle, Washington
Contributors: Chuck and Addie

Motore Coffee
1904 9th Avenue
Seattle, Washington
www.motorecoffee.com
Contributors: DJ and Scott

Online Coffee Company
1404 E Pine Street, 1720 E Olive Way,
& 1111 1st Avenue
Seattle, Washington
www.onlinecoffeeco.com
Contributor: Kyle

Sleepless Coffee
2255 Harbor Avenue SW
Seattle, Washington
107 S. 3rd Street
Renton, Washington
www.sleeplesscoffee.com
Contributors: Carri and Diana

Stumptown Coffee Roasters
7 locations in Portland and Seattle
www.stumptowncoffee.com
Contributors: Duane, Aaron, Kyle, and Matthew

Top Pot Doughnuts
609 Summit Avenue E., 2124 5th Avenue,
& 6855 35th Avenue NE
Seattle, Washington
www.toppotdoughnuts.com
Contributors: Kim and Christine

Tougo Coffee Co.
1410 18th Avenue
Seattle, Washington
www.tougocoffee.com
Contributor: Brian

Trabant Coffee & Chai
1309 NE 45th Street & 602 2nd Avenue
Seattle, Washington
www.trabantcoffee.com
Contributor: Tatiana and Lorrie

Uptown Espresso
7 locations in Seattle
www.uptownespresso.net
Contributors: Dow and Orion

Vérité Coffee
2052 Market Street, 1101 34th Avenue,
& 4556 California Avenue SW
Seattle, Washington
www.veritecoffee.com
Contributors: Jody, Jen, Wendy, Tessa, Rebecca,
and Curtis

Victrola Coffee
411 15th Avenue E. & 310 E. Pike Street
Seattle, Washington
www.victrolacoffee.com
Contributors: Jen, Chris, Tonya, Kelleen,
and Karen

Zoka Coffee Roaster & Tea Company
2200 N. 56th Street
& 2901 NE Blakeley Street
Seattle, Washington
7811 SE Center Boulevard
Snoqualmie, Washington
www.zokacoffee.com
Contributor: Aimee

Acknowledgments

Dani would like to thank everyone who participated in and contributed to this book. It was great fun and we appreciate all of your help! Thanks to Chris and his impeccable design, skills, hard work, and patience. A big thanks to Terence Maikels, and all at Sasquatch Books, for making the book come to life. Thank you to family and friends for all of your support. And, of course, an enormous thank you to coffee drinkers everywhere (especially my amazing customers at Fuel!) who have allowed me to make a career out of a daily cup of joe. I appreciate you all!

Chris would like to thank Dani, whose sincerity and passion were an inspiration and whose encouragement and support were very important during creation of this book. He would also like to thank Terence, Liza, Sarah, Kate, and Rosebud at Sasquatch Books, Julie Poole, and all the great coffee shops that took the time to submit such amazing content to this project. Finally, huge thanks go to the three designers that contributed many of the layouts in this book: Jean Bradbury, Aileen Morrow, and Leslie Riibe. Their skills and efforts helped this turn out much better than I could have imagined.

About Dani and Chris

Dani Cone has been a barista in the Northwest for more than 15 years. In July 2006, she opened her first Fuel coffee shop in Seattle, and has since opened two more shops. Her writings have appeared in such publications as *The Stranger*. She lives in Seattle.

Chris Munson is a graphic designer living and working in Seattle. He has a degree in graphic design and illustration from Seattle Central Community College, and he consumed a lot of coffee during the creation of this book. Visit his website at www.cmunsondesign.com.